Deadly Snakes

Tracey Turner

LONDON·SYDNEY

Warning! This is not a normal book!

First published in 2013 by
Franklin Watts
338 Euston Road
London NW1 3BH

Franklin Watts Australia
Level 17/207 Kent Street
Sydney NSW 2000

Series editor: Adrian Cole
Art direction: Peter Scoulding
Editor: Paul Rockett
Design: D R Ink
Picture research: Diana Morris

Acknowledgements:
Beyondimages/istockphoto: 13.
Oliver Born/Biosphotos/FLPA: 6.
Dinodia/Alamy: 22.
Andrea & Antonella Ferran/NHPA/Photoshot: 10.
five spots/Shutterstock: front cover b, back cover t.
Michael Fogden/NHPA/Photoshot: 19.
Michael & Patricia Fogden/FLPA: 5.
Four Oaks/Shutterstock: 23.
Ken Griffiths/NHPA/Photoshot: 4, 17.
Eric Isselee/Shutterstock: 16. Mg Kuipers/Dreamstime: 7.
Martin Van Lokven/Minden Pictures/FLPA: 21.
Chris Mattison/FLPA: 14. Jay Ondriella/Shutterstock: 15.
Pete Oxford/Minden Pictures/FLPA: 11.
Paytai/Shutterstock: front cover t. Robert Pickett/Papilio/Alamy: 18.
Wolfgang Poelzer/Alamy: 20. Stu Porter/Shutterstock: 12.
reptiles4all/Shutterstock: 9. Martin Willis/Minden Pictures/FLPA: 8.
Every attempt has been made to clear copyright.
Should there be any inadvertent omission please
apply to the publisher for rectification.

A CIP catalogue record for this book
is available from the British Library.

Dewey Classification: 629.2'221

(hb) ISBN: 978 1 4451 1449 1
(Library ebook) ISBN: 978 1 4451 2510 7

Printed in China

Franklin Watts is a division of Hachette
Children's Books, an Hachette UK company.
www.hachette.co.uk

Contents

Ultimate 20 is not just a book where you can find out loads of facts and stats about fantastic stuff – it's also a brilliant game book!

How to play

1. Grab a copy of *Ultimate 20* – oh, you have. OK, now get your friends to grab a copy, too.

2. Each player closes their eyes and flicks to a game page. Now, open your eyes and choose one of the Ultimate 20. Decide who goes first, then that person reads out which snake they've chosen, plus the name of the stat. For example, this player has chosen the Puff Adder and the Length of fangs stat, with an Ultimate 20 ranking of 5.

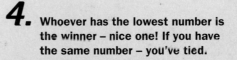

Most dangerous: 13
Length of fangs: 33 mm 5
Venom yield: 100–350 mg 8
Length: 1 m 16
Rarity: Least concern 10

3. Now, challenge your friends to see who has the highest-ranking stat – the lower the number (from 1–20) the better your chances of winning. (1 = good, 20 = goofy.)

Player 1

Most dangerous: 5

Player 2

Most dangerous: 4

4. Whoever has the lowest number is the winner – nice one! If you have the same number – you've tied.

Time to flick, choose, challenge again!

(If you land on the same game page, choose the Ultimate 20 listing opposite.)

Mash it up!

If you haven't got the same *Ultimate 20* book as your friends, you can **STILL** play — Ultimate 20 Mash Up! The rules are the same as the regular game (above), so flick and choose one of your Ultimate 20 and a stat, then read out them out. Each player does this. Now read out the Ultimate 20 ranking to see whose choice is the best. Can Julius Caesar beat a werewolf? Can an Aston Martin One-77 beat a cannon?

Inland Taipan

The inland taipan, also known as the "fierce snake", is the world's most venomous snake. The poison delivered in a single bite is enough to kill 100 people, and it can kill an adult human in less than an hour.

Deadly hunter

The inland taipan isn't brightly coloured or patterned – it's usually dark brown or olive green, and about two metres long. They are found in the grasslands and plains of central Australia, where they eat small mammals. They kill their prey quickly, injecting around 40,000 times the amount of venom required to kill one average-sized mouse.

Small fangs

Although the inland taipan's venom is the most toxic snake venom in the world, the snake isn't one of the world's most dangerous to people. Despite its nickname, the snake isn't aggressive – unless cornered or threatened – and its fangs are short. The snake is also quite rare and it doesn't live near people. In fact, there are no recorded human deaths from an inland taipan's bite – not one!

Most dangerous: 2

Length of fangs: 3.5–6.2 mm 13

Venom yield: 44–110 mg 12

Length: 1.8 m 11

Rarity: Data deficient 6

Bushmaster

Bushmasters are the longest venomous snakes in the Western Hemisphere. They also hold the record for being the largest pit viper in the world. Both these things make the bushmaster one of the most-feared South American snakes.

Most dangerous:

Length of fangs: 25 mm

Venom yield: 200–500 mg

Length: 2–2.5 m

Rarity: Vulnerable

14
4
5
7
2

Jungle camouflage

Bushmasters live in remote rainforest areas of Central and South America. In their jungle habitat they're extremely well camouflaged, ranging from reddish brown to pinkish grey, with dark brown or black triangular patterns along their bodies. Bushmasters are usually about 2 m long, but the longest ever recorded was more than 3.5 m long. (That's as long as a small car.)

Venomous vipers

Like other pit vipers (such as the common lancehead on page 21), bushmasters have heat sensitive pits between their eyes and their nostrils which can detect warm-blooded animals. The snakes lie in wait before striking, and inject a large quantity of venom through their fangs, which instantly immobilises their prey. A bushmaster bite could easily kill a human, but they live in remote rainforests, away from people. However, it's not all good news. Victims of a bushmaster bite are often a long way from medical help, and so most people who are bitten die.

King Cobra

King cobras are the world's longest venomous snake, up to 5.5 m long (as long as a big car). They can deliver enough venom in a single bite to kill 20 people.

Hooded menace

When threatened, a king cobra can raise a third of its body length up off the ground – that's up to about 1.8 m, taller than most adult men – and it can still move forwards! Like all cobras, it can expand its neck into a hood, plus it has a low hiss, like the growl of a dog. This terrifying combination makes the king cobra the most fearsome snake of all!

Most dangerous:

Length of fangs: 10 mm

Venom yield: 350–500 mg

Length: 4–5.5 m

Rarity: Vulnerable

8
14
4
4
2

Shy snakes

Despite its menacing appearance, the king cobra isn't responsible for many human deaths. This is mainly because it doesn't share the same habitat as people. It lives in the rainforests and plains of Southeast Asia, China and India, where it preys on other snakes, as well as mammals, lizards and eggs. It avoids contact with people wherever possible, but it can be aggressive when threatened.

Black Mamba

Black mambas are among the most feared snakes in Africa. They're big, fast and extremely venomous.

Black jaws

Oddly, black mambas aren't black in colour, they're usually brown or grey. The insides of their mouths are black though, and they display these when threatened. They are the longest venomous snake in Africa, and the second longest in the world.

Speedy snakes

Black mambas are the world's fastest snake. They can reach speeds of up to 20 km per hour, which, for a creature with no legs, is very fast indeed! But don't worry, they use this speed to get away from humans rather than chase them.

Most dangerous: | 1
Length of fangs: 4 mm | 16
Venom yield: 120 mg | 11
Length: 4.3 m | 3
Rarity: Least concern | 10

Kiss of death

Black mambas are aggressive when threatened, and are especially feared because they deliver a large amount of venom with each bite. This is on average 120 mg per bite, but can sometimes be as high as 400 mg. Without the antivenom, almost 100 per cent of victims die – the world's highest snakebite death rate.

7

Tiger Snake

The tiger snake is one of the most venomous snakes in the world – death can occur within 30 minutes of being bitten!

Most dangerous: 12
Length of fangs: 3.5 mm 17
Venom yield: 250 mg 6
Length: 2.9 m 5
Rarity: Least concern 10

Stripy tigers

There are various different kinds of tiger snake. They can be brown, grey, olive green or black in colour. Some, but not all, are striped with yellow bands, which gives the snakes their name. All of the different types of tiger snake are extremely venomous. They're found in the southern half of Australia, including its islands, usually near the coast. They feed on small mammals, frogs and birds. However, sometimes they're found looking for food in suburban areas, which can bring them into contact with lots of people.

Forked tongue

Tiger snakes have an extremely sensitive forked tongue that helps them locate their prey. Their forked tongue acts as a brush, picking up molecules that it transfers to the roof of its mouth – this is where a snake's sense of smell and taste is located. A fork-shaped tongue is able to check out a larger area than most other shaped tongues, allowing snakes to track down their prey more quickly.

Gaboon Viper

The Gaboon viper is famous for its record-breaking fangs which can grow up to 55 mm long! It also delivers between 450–600 mg of venom in one bite – the highest amount of any snake in the world.

Fatal fangs

The Gaboon viper lives in the rainforest and savanna of Africa. It usually grows to about 1 m long, though the longest one recorded was more than 2 m long. These snakes have thick, heavy bodies, which are usually pale brown with darker brown, triangular markings. The shape of their head – a bit like a leaf – and their colouring makes them blend into the forest floor, where they ambush small mammals. Although the Gaboon viper's venom is not one of the most powerful snake venoms in the world, they deliver a lot of it with their record-breaking fangs.

Most dangerous:	11
Length of fangs: 55 mm	1
Venom yield: 450–600 mg	3
Length: 1–1.5 m	14
Rarity: Data deficient	6

Death bite

Gaboon vipers can be found on farmland, near where people live and work. They're not usually aggressive, but when they bite their prey they tend to hang on to it until the animal is dead. This means that if they bite a human, they're unlikely to let go until they've injected a deadly amount of venom.

Spectacled Cobra

The spectacled cobra, also known as the Indian cobra, is one of the "big four" snakes: the four kinds of snake responsible for the most snakebite deaths in India.

Spectacled hood

Like all cobras, the spectacled cobra can open out the ribs on its neck into a hood when it feels threatened. The snake gets its name because of the pattern on the back of its hood, which looks a bit like a pair of spectacles. It's usually brown and preys on rats, frogs and other small creatures, including other snakes. The snake is found in India, Nepal, Bangladesh, Sri Lanka and Pakistan. It lives in a variety of habitats, from plains and jungles to the outskirts of towns, where it regularly comes into contact with people.

Most dangerous:

Length of fangs: 10 mm

Venom yield: 250 mg

Length: 1.9 m

Rarity: Vulnerable

4
8
6
10
2

Snakes in the house

In India, the spectacled cobra is often found entering people's homes in search of food. This close proximity means that many people are bitten. However, bite victims who don't receive any medical attention can still survive. The spectacled cobra usually delivers a warning bite first, and this may not contain any venom – it's known as a "dry bite". Just don't hang around for the second bite...

Green Anaconda

The green anaconda is the world's biggest snake, and is the only snake in the *Ultimate 20* that is not venomous. Instead, it uses the muscle power of its coils to crush prey to death.

Green giants

Green anacondas can be up to 9 m long. They aren't as long as their close relations, the pythons, but they have much thicker bodies. They can also weigh almost twice as much – up to 230 kg! Green anacondas live in the swamps and rivers of South America's tropical rainforests, where they feed on all sorts of animals, including very large ones such as wild pigs, deer and even jaguars.

Squeezing snakes

Green anacondas kill their prey by squeezing it tighter and tighter in their massive, powerful coils, until it can't breathe. Although their heads are often much smaller than the prey they eat, green anacondas have special ligaments in their jaws that allow the snake to swallow big creatures whole. They're capable of killing a human being, but reports of attacks on people are extremely rare – probably because very few people live near anacondas.

Most dangerous:	20
Length of fangs: 0	20
Venom yield: 0	20
Length: 6–9 m	1
Rarity: Data deficient	6

Puff Adder

The deadly puff adder kills more people in Africa than any other snake, partly because they are quite common. They will also stand their ground instead of running away when they are approached.

Most dangerous: 13

Length of fangs: 33 mm   5

Venom yield: 100–350 mg   8

Length: 1 m   16

Rarity: Least concern   10

Nocturnal hunters

Puff adders are found in dry, rocky grasslands throughout most of Africa, as well as in Saudi Arabia and Yemen. They are large snakes: usually around 1 m long, and thick around the middle. Their markings vary according to where they're found, but most are yellow or orange with grey or dark brown triangular patterns along their back. During the day they're often found basking in the Sun alongside paths, where they can be hard to spot. They hunt at night for small creatures including rats, frogs, lizards and birds.

Large litters

The majority of snakes lay eggs, but some, like the puff adder, give birth to live young. In fact, the puff adder gives birth to more live young than any other snake. The female produces an average litter of around 50 young. However there is a record of one female giving birth to 156 baby snakes!

Coastal Taipan

After the inland taipan and the eastern brown snake, the coastal taipan is the world's third most venomous land snake. It's also the largest venomous snake in Australia.

What a whopper!

These reddish-brown, black or olive-coloured snakes live near the coasts of New Guinea and Northern Australia. They have good eyesight, and often hunt with their heads raised, on the lookout for their prey of small mammals and birds. Most of them are between 1.2–2 m long, but the largest recorded coastal taipan was nearly 3 m long!

Venom effects

Like most snakes, coastal taipans avoid humans when they can. However, if provoked they will gather their body into loose coils and strike quickly, inflicting multiple bites. The effects of the venom can be rapid, causing headaches, vomiting, muscle weakness and kidney failure. If untreated, death can occur around 90 minutes after being bitten.

Most dangerous:	7
Length of fangs: 12 mm	7
Venom yield: 120–400 mg	6
Length: 1.2–2 m	17
Rarity: Data deficient	6

Russell's Viper

Russell's viper is one of the "big four" snakes, responsible for the most human deaths by snakebite. It's found throughout India and Southeast Asia and parts of China, where it often comes into contact with people.

Snakes next door

Russell's viper is brownish in colour, with dark oval or diamond-shaped patterns along its thick body. It lives in grasslands, scrublands and on farms, where they hunt various small creatures, but especially rats – which is why they are also found in towns.

Most dangerous:

Length of fangs: 16 mm

Venom yield: 130–250 mg

Length: 1–1.5 m

Rarity: Least concern

6
6
7
14
10

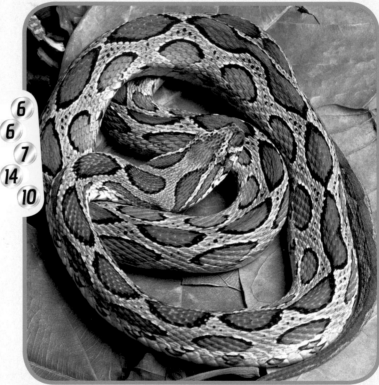

Death toll

There are more cases of Russell's viper bites during the time of year when rice is planted and harvested. Rats are common in rice fields, and this attracts Russell's vipers into the fields. When they feel threatened, the snakes coil into a series of "S" shapes and hiss very loudly. The snake can strike quickly, and it can deliver around 130–250 mg of very powerful venom. The snakes are the cause of thousands of deaths per year. Along with the spectacled cobra, they are responsible for more human deaths than any other snake in the world.

Eastern Coral Snake

This brightly coloured, highly venomous snake is one of the most feared in the Southeastern United States. They spend most of their time in underground burrows or piles of leaves, and hunt lizards, frogs and smaller snakes.

Most dangerous: 19

Length of fangs: 1.6–2.7 mm 19

Venom yield: 2–20 mg 15

Length: 51–76 cm 20

Rarity: Least concern 10

Colourful corals

Eastern coral snakes live in wooded and marshy areas in the south-east of the United States. The snakes are up to about 75 cm long and have bright red, black and yellow bands around their bodies. Some non-venomous snakes look like eastern coral snakes, and people have made up rhymes to tell the difference: 'Red on yellow, kill a fellow, red on black, friend of Jack'. But in fact people don't have much to fear...

Snakebite survival

Although the snake's venom is powerful, not much of it is injected in a single bite. People rarely get bitten by eastern coral snakes – the snakes aren't aggressive, and usually only bite if they're handled or stepped on. There haven't been any recorded human deaths since the 1960s, when an antivenom was developed.

Eastern Diamondback Rattlesnake

Measuring up to 2.5 m long, the eastern diamondback rattlesnake is the largest venomous snake in North America. They are famous for the rattle at the end of their tail.

Death rattle

The snakes are named for their markings: they have a striking yellow-bordered diamond pattern on their backs. When threatened, they make their famous rattle by shaking the end of their tails, which are made of hollow segments. Eastern diamondbacks live in the south-east of the United States, in sandy or pine woodlands and coastal areas. They hunt rats and other small mammals.

Most dangerous:

Length of fangs: 25 mm

Venom yield: 200–850 mg

Length: 2.5 m

Rarity: Least concern

9
5
1
6
10

Shedding skin

Snakes shed their skin by rubbing themselves against hard objects, like rocks. They shed their skin to allow for growth and to remove any parasites that may be living on them. Rattlesnakes shed their skin several times a year, gaining a new rattle segment with each new skin. Adult rattlesnakes can have fangs that measure up to 25 mm long and they are known to shed these every 6–10 weeks.

Eastern Brown Snake

The eastern brown snake has the second most toxic venom of all land snakes. They are the cause of most snakebite deaths in Australia.

Close contact

These snakes live in eastern Australia, from the mountains to the coast, usually in dry grasslands and woodlands. However, their population is also increasing in urban areas where there are plenty of rats for them to eat. They are also drawn to farms and barns in search of food, which is great news for farmers! The snakes are long, up to 2 m, although most are around 1.5 m long. They can be shades of brown, orange or grey. Females lay an average of 15 eggs, which can take 36–95 days to hatch depending on the surrounding temperature.

Surving a bite

Although the fangs of the eastern brown snake are short, and usually only release a small amount of venom, it is important to treat each bite as potentially lethal. To survive a fatal bite it is important to get hold of the necessary antivenom. This should be injected into a vein, with a dose lasting from 15–30 minutes. Side-effects from the antivenom may require the patient to rest for up to four days.

Most dangerous:	
	10
Length of fangs: 2.8 mm	17
Venom yield: 4–10 mg	16
Length: 1.5–2 m	9
Rarity: Least concern	10

Saw-scaled Viper

The saw-scaled viper, also called the carpet viper, is another snake listed as one of the "big four" most dangerous snakes. It is responsible for killing thousands of people every year.

Most dangerous: 4

Length of fangs: 3–5 mm 16

Venom yield: 5–48 mg 18

Length: 40–80 cm 18

Rarity: Least concern 10

Rasping scales

There are eight different kinds of saw-scaled viper. These live in the deserts and dry plains of West Africa, the Middle East and South Asia, with large populations in India and Sri Lanka. They can be 35 cm to just under 1 m long, and their colour varies to blend in with the surroundings – they might be sandy yellow, brown or grey, with blotches or bands around their thick bodies. They get their name from the serrated scales on their lower bodies, which they rub together when threatened, making a rasping sound like a saw.

Super sidewinding

Saw-scaled vipers are one of a few snakes which move by sidewinding. Sidewinding involves looping the body in a slanting position so that only two points are in contact with the ground at any one time. The movement leaves behind a "J"-shaped trail and prevents the body from overheating due to excessive contact with the hot desert sand.

Death Adder

Death adders have one of the most powerful snake venoms in the world, and hold the world record for the quickest strike of any snake at 0.15 seconds. But they don't live up to their terrifying name, in fact, they were thought to have originally been called "deaf adders".

Adder family

There are several different species of death adder, but none of them are actually from the adder family (vipers). Instead, death adders are elapids, a group of snakes that have hollow fixed fangs they inject their venom through. Death adders live in Australia, Tasmania and New Guinea, and are up to about 75 cm long. They can be various colours, usually with broad bands around their thick bodies.

Killer venom

Death adders don't come into contact with people very often. This is just as well, as their venom contains neurotoxins that can kill a human within a few hours of being bitten. Luckily, an antivenom is available and so reported deaths are now rare.

Luring its victims

Death adders have thin, worm-like tips to their tails, which they twitch to lure small animals. The snakes lurk – hidden in sand, soil, or amongst leaves – waiting for an animal to investigate the wriggling tail tip. Then they strike with lightning-fast speed, biting quick with their 6 mm-long fangs.

Most dangerous:	15
Length of fangs: 6 mm	11
Venom yield: 40–100 mg	13
Length: 75 cm	19
Rarity: Least concern	10

Beaked Sea Snake

The venom of a beaked sea snake is one of the most toxic snake venoms in the world. It's responsible for nine out of ten human deaths from sea snake bites.

Most dangerous: **18**

Length of fangs: 4 mm **16**

Venom yield: 7.7–9 mg **18**

Length: 1.4 m **15**

Rarity: Least concern **10**

Deep diving
Beaked sea snakes are grey with darker grey bands along their bodies. They live in mangrove swamps, estuaries and coastal waters of the Western Pacific and Indian Oceans, where they swim close to the bottom, preying on catfish and prawns. They're capable of diving down to 100 m below the surface, and can stay underwater for five hours between breaths.

Underwater assassin
Even though the snake's fangs are just 4 mm long, its venom is so powerful that just 1.5 mg is enough to kill an adult human. In fact, there's enough venom in one bite to kill 52 men! Many sea snakes have extremely powerful venom, but the beaked sea snake is also highly aggressive. It will strike if someone gets too close, such as when a fisherman wades into murky water.

Common Lancehead

The common lancehead is highly venomous, and the most dangerous snake to people in tropical Central and South America. The snake gets its name from its triangular head, shaped like a lance.

Yellow beard

In Spanish, the common lancehead is known as *barba amarilla*, which means "yellow beard", because the underside of its head is sometimes yellow. The snakes vary in colour and markings – brown, grey and olive-green, with or without darker blotches or diamond shapes – to blend in with their forest floor habitat. They prey on small mammals and sense their location with a special sensory pit between their eye and nostril, a common feature with other pit vipers.

Most dangerous: **17**
Length of fangs: 2.5 mm **18**
Venom yield: 124 mg **14**
Length: 2 m **8**
Rarity: Critically endangered **1**

Super scales

The scales on a snake help them to move easily over the ground without any friction. The arrangement of scales is often used to help identify snake species. The scales are arranged in rows – the common lancehead has around 21–29 rows of scales around its mid-body.

Common Krait

The common krait is another "big four" snake, killing thousands of people in India, Bangladesh, Pakistan and Sri Lanka every year.

Most dangerous:

Length of fangs: 36 mm

Venom yield: 10 mg

Length: 0.9–1.75 m

Rarity: Vulnerable

5
4
17
12
2

Night hunters

The common krait, also known as the Indian or blue krait, is usually just under 1 m long, though it can grow to nearly twice that length. The snakes are black or bluish-black, usually with thin white bands along the length of their bodies. They hunt at night, feeding on other snakes, including other common kraits, as well as frogs and lizards.

Stealthy strike

Common kraits often share their habitat with humans – on farms and in towns and villages. Very few people are bitten by these snakes, but those that are don't always know they've been bitten. The snakes are nocturnal and their bite isn't painful, so a victim of a common krait might not wake up after having been bitten!

Boomslang

The boomslang is a tree-dwelling snake from Africa. It is highly feared because of its hemotoxic venom, which stops blood from clotting, and can cause bite victims to bleed to death.

Tree snake

Boomslang means "tree snake" in Afrikaans. Their colouring varies, but they are often green with black markings (usually males) or brown (usually females) – both colours act as good camouflage amongst branches and leaves. They prey on lizards and birds, and sometimes small mammals. They hunt in bushes and trees and are able to hang outstretched from tree branches to ambush their prey.

Most dangerous:
Length of fangs: 3–5 mm   16
Venom yield: 1.6–8 mg   16
Length: 1–1.6 m   19
Rarity: Least concern   13
10

Colubridae snake family

Boomslangs belong to the colubridae snake family. This is the largest family of snakes. Many snakes in this family have their fangs towards the back of their jaws and are non-venomous or have venom which is not harmful to humans. The boomslang, however, is an exception to this family. It can open its jaws up to 170 degrees when biting, releasing a venom which, though slow to show effects, is deadly.

Glossary

Afrikaans – a language used in South Africa

aggressive – likely to attack

antivenom – a serum which acts against the effects of venom

camouflaged – blending in with its surroundings

habitat – a natural environment or home of a variety of plants and animals

hemotoxic – poisons that destroy blood

immobilise – make unable to move

ligament – tough stretchy tissue that connects bones together

neurotoxin – a poison that acts on an animal's nervous system

nocturnal – active during the night rather than the day

parasite – a living thing that lives off other living things

savanna – a flat grassland

suburban the area of a city or town outside the central area

sensory – relating to the senses

serrated – having a saw-like edge

toxic – poisonous

venom – poisonous fluid produced by snakes and other stinging animals and injected into prey or other animals

Western Hemisphere – the half of the Earth containing the Americas

Index